AMAZING
Amusement
Park Rides

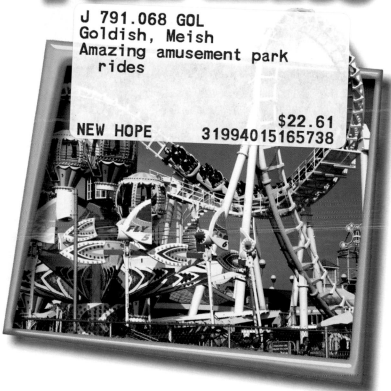

by Meish Goldish

Consultants: Eric Gieszl
Editor and Founder of ultimaterollercoaster.com

Dave Hahner
Historian for American Coaster Enthusiasts

BEARPORT
PUBLISHING

New York, New York

Credits

Cover and Title Page, © Racheal Grazias/Shutterstock; TOC, © David Acosta Allely/Shutterstock; 4T, Courtesy of The Library of Congress Prints and Photographs Division; 4B, © The Granger Collection, New York; 5, © North Wind Picture Archives/Alamy; 6, © Joel A. Rogers/CoasterGallery.com; 7, © Joel A. Rogers/CoasterGallery.com; 8, © Asia File/Alamy; 9, © Paul Russell/Corbis; 10, Courtesy of Dreamworld/WhiteWater World; 11, © LatitudeStock/Brian Garrett; 12, © Tracey Stivers; 13, Courtesy of Kings Island; 14, © Adam Sandy/2003 UltimateRollercoaster.com; 15, © Adam Sandy/2003 UltimateRollercoaster.com; 16, Courtesy of www.themeparkreview.com; 17, © Andrea Lipinski; 18, © Science Faction/SuperStock; 19, © UPI Photo Service/Newscom; 20, Courtesy of Beach Park; 21, © Ana Muniz; 22A, © CB2/ZOB/WENN/Newscom; 22B, © John R. Kreul/Independent Picture Service/Alamy; 22C, © Brian Wright/Commorancy on Flickr; 22D, Courtesy of Peter Gugerell; 23, © Racheal Grazias/Shutterstock.

Publisher: Kenn Goin
Editorial Director: Adam Siegel
Creative Director: Spencer Brinker
Photo Researcher: James O'Connor

Library of Congress Cataloging-in-Publication Data

Goldish, Meish.
    Amazing amusement park rides / by Meish Goldish ; consultant, Eric Gieszl.
        p. cm. — (So big compared to what?)
    Includes bibliographical references and index.
    ISBN-13: 978-1-61772-304-9 (library binding)
    ISBN-10: 1-61772-304-5 (library binding)
    1. Amusement rides—Juvenile literature. I. Gieszl, Eric. II. Title.
    GV1859.G65 2012
    791.06'8—dc22
                                2011009353

For more information, write to Bearport Publishing Company, Inc., 45 West 21st Street, Suite 3B, New York, New York 10010. Printed in the United States of America.

10 9 8 7 6 5 4 3

CONTENTS

BIG THRILLS

Every year, **amusement parks** offer bigger, faster, and taller rides. Back in the 1880s, one of America's first roller coasters, the Gravity Pleasure Switchback Railway, was only 50 feet (15 m) high and traveled just six miles per hour (9.7 kph). At that speed, many adults could outrun it. Today, some coasters are nearly ten times as tall and more than 20 times as fast!

At its highest point, the Gravity Pleasure Switchback Railway was only as tall as nine adults standing on one another's shoulders.

The Gravity Pleasure Switchback Railway opened at Coney Island in Brooklyn, New York, in 1884.

Other rides have also grown. In 1893, the first Ferris wheel was introduced at a world's fair in Chicago. The wheel rose 264 feet (80 m) into the air. It amazed people at the time. Yet the largest Ferris wheel today is more than double that size!

In this book you will discover some of the world's biggest, fastest—and scariest—amusement park **attractions**. You will also find out how their size and weight compare to other spectacular sights. So hold on tight—it's going to be an amazing ride!

The first Ferris wheel was as high as a 26-story building.

The Ferris wheel was invented by George W. Ferris. It is the only amusement park ride that is named for its inventor.

STEEL DRAGON 2000

Opened: 2000   **Where:** Nagashima Spa Land in Mie, Japan   **Length:** 8,133 feet (2,479 m)

Amazing Feature: World's longest roller-coaster track

Roller-coaster lovers like to zoom fast and far. They get to do both on Steel Dragon 2000. It's the longest roller coaster in the world. The winding track runs 8,133 feet (2,479 m). If it were laid out in one long straight line, the track would stretch across 27 football fields placed end to end!

Passengers on Steel Dragon 2000 zoom along the lengthy track at 95 miles per hour (153 kph). That's faster than the average speed of an Acela—Amtrak's high-speed train. At the Steel Dragon 2000's lightning **pace**, the entire ride takes only about four minutes to complete.

Steel Dragon 2000 takes passengers along many curves and drops during the ride.

The roller-coaster track rises 318 feet (97 m) high—almost twice the height of the giant ocean liner the *Titanic*.

Steel Dragon got its name because it is made of steel and opened in 2000, the Asian Year of the Dragon.

THE SINGAPORE FLYER

Opened: 2008   **Where:** Marina Centre in Singapore   **Height:** 541 feet (165 m)

Amazing Feature: World's tallest Ferris wheel

Steel Dragon 2000 offers a long, exciting ride. For the highest thrill, however, riders must hop on the Singapore Flyer. It's the tallest Ferris wheel in the world. Located in Singapore, an island country in Southeast Asia, this gigantic **structure** rises 541 feet (165 m)—taller than the height of the Great Pyramid in Egypt!

Riders on the Singapore Flyer sit in air-conditioned **capsules**. Each of the 28 capsules is big enough to hold 28 people. That means 784 passengers can ride on the giant wheel at once. That's nearly one and a half times the number of passengers that fit in a large Boeing 747-400 airplane!

Each capsule is 23 feet (7 m) long. That's big enough for four adults to lie down on the seat and stretch out head to toe.

8

Riders at the top of the Ferris wheel can see for a distance of 28 miles (45 km)—far enough to view parts of two other Asian countries, Malaysia and Indonesia.

It takes 32 minutes for the Singapore Flyer to complete one full **rotation**.

THE GIANT DROP

Opened: 1998   **Where:** Dreamworld
in Queensland, Australia   **Height:** 390 feet (119 m)

Amazing Feature: World's tallest drop tower ride

For some amusement park fans, the only thing more thrilling than riding high is falling fast. That's exactly what riders do on the Giant Drop. Sitting in a **gondola**, they're lifted for 90 seconds to the top of a 390-foot (119-m) tower. Then the passengers brace themselves for the excitement about to come.

Whoosh! The gondola suddenly drops down the tower. Riders fall at 84 miles per hour (135 kph). That's faster than the top speed limit for cars on a highway! In just five quick seconds, passengers are back at the base of the tower. Many people say it feels almost like skydiving—and you don't even have to get on a plane.

Magnetic brakes stop the gondola from hitting the ground at the end of the drop. The brakes are designed to last more than a million years.

The 390-foot (119-m) tower is about 85 feet (26 m) taller than the Statue of Liberty.

The Giant Drop is the tallest and fastest **drop ride** in the world.

SLINGSHOT

Opened: 2002   **Where:** Kings Island in Mason, Ohio   **Height:** 275 feet (84 m)

Amazing Feature: Flying steel basket

If dropping fast is a thrill, imagine what flying straight up into the air is like. To find out, just ask passengers on SlingShot. Two riders sit inside a steel basket. It's attached with steel ropes to two tall towers. A powerful **electromagnet** holds the basket down on the ground. When the magnet is turned off, the fun begins.

Suddenly, the steel basket shoots straight into the air. It reaches a height of 275 feet (84 m). That's higher than 27 basketball poles stacked on top of one another! The ropes hold the basket as it bounces wildly in the air. Riders are tossed around until the basket slowly comes to a rest. The unforgettable excitement lasts three minutes.

Two SlingShot passengers get ready to fly through the air.

The basket shoots upward at nearly 100 miles per hour (161 kph)—three times as fast as an eagle soaring through the air.

Each tower stands 180 feet (55 m) high. That's about as tall as 30 adult men standing on top of one another.

SlingShot is a type of ride known as a reverse **bungee jump.** A bungee jumper travels from a higher level to a lower one, but a SlingShot rider does just the opposite.

DELIRIUM

Opened: 2003   **Where:** Kings Island in Mason, Ohio   **Height:** 137 feet (42 m)

Amazing Feature: Giant spinning wheel

Imagine flying in the air on a giant spinning wheel. That's the thrill that riders experience on Delirium. The ride is shaped like a huge giraffe. Each of the four long legs is 85 feet (26 m) high. That's 14 times as tall as the legs on a real giraffe!

Delirium's riders sit on the outside of a giant wheel. It's located at the end of the "giraffe's" long neck, where the head would be. As the neck rocks back and forth, the wheel spins around and around. Riders swing as high as 137 feet (42 m)— nearly twice the height of the White House!

The huge wheel on Delirium is called the Giant Frisbee. Up to 50 people can ride on it at one time.

Riders swing up to 76 miles per hour (122 kph). That's faster than the world's fastest land animal—the cheetah—can run.

The word *delirium* means wild, uncontrollable excitement. The ride was given that name because passengers feel extremely excited while swinging wildly.

THE CRYPT

Opened: 2005   **Where:** Kings Dominion in Doswell, Virginia   **Height:** 60 feet (18 m)

Amazing Feature: Shooting water geysers

Some park rides do more than swing their passengers. They flip them over as well. The Crypt is a giant swing that is ready to do just that. It has a long gondola that can hold 38 riders sitting back to back in two rows. It **hovers** over a steamy pool of water with **geysers** just waiting to explode.

When the ride begins, passengers swing upward 60 feet (18 m). That's one and a half times as high as a football goalpost. The Crypt then flips passengers over completely, so that they are turned upside-down in the air. Each time the riders flip, geysers from the pool shoot water straight up. As if that isn't enough, flames burst into the air—just out of reach so that no one gets scorched.

The Crypt weighs about 80 tons (73 metric tons)— about as heavy as 12 large African elephants.

About 760 passengers can ride the Crypt each hour. That's enough to fill up ten school buses.

JURASSIC PARK: THE RIDE

Opened: 1996   **Where:** Universal Studios Hollywood in Los Angeles, California   **Length:** 1,900 feet (579 m)

Amazing Feature: 84-foot (26-m) drop

In the movie *Jurassic Park*, scientists brought dinosaurs back to life. How can you see these giant beasts in the real world? Just ask people who've taken an amazing adventure on Jurassic Park: The Ride. Passengers sit in a **raft** that moves along a track running through water. The track is 1,900 feet (579 m) long. That's longer than six football fields placed end to end!

During the five-and-a-half-minute ride, passengers travel through a **model** jungle called Jurassic Park. It's based on the movie of the same name. Riders see many huge dinosaurs along the way. Near the end of the ride, the raft suddenly **plunges** 84 feet (26 m) into a **lagoon** to escape an angry *T. rex*. It's like falling off an eight-story building!

The ride uses 1.5 million gallons (5.7 million liters) of water. That's about as much water as a town of 15,000 people uses in one day!

Riders are threatened by a *T. rex* that stands 50 feet (15 m) high. That's three times as tall as a real *T. rex!*

The movie *Jurassic Park* opened in 1993, three years before the ride.

INSANO

Opened: 1989   **Where:** Beach Park in Ceará, Brazil   **Height:** 135 feet (41 m)

Amazing Feature: World's tallest water slide

Some thrill-seekers want to do more than sit in a raft on the water. They want to be in the water themselves. If they take a ride down the Insano, they're in luck. This giant water slide is 135 feet (41 m) high. Riders zoom down the **chute** at 65 miles per hour (105 kph)—faster than a horse racing around a track. Happily, they end up in a comfortable pool of water at the bottom of the slide.

What new and more amazing rides will amusement parks offer in the years ahead? Only time will tell. One thing, however, is certain: There will always be plenty of brave people willing to ride them!

Insano holds the Guinness World Record as the tallest water slide in the world.

At 135 feet (41 m) tall, the drop from the top of Insano to the pool below is more than the drop from the top of Niagara Falls to the rocks below.

Riders travel down the water slide so quickly that the ride is over in only four or five seconds.

MORE AMAZING AMUSEMENT PARK RIDES

Many amazing amusement park rides are found around the world. Here are four others.

Macau Tower

One of the world's tallest bungee jumps is the Macau Tower in Macau, China. Speeding along at 124 miles per hour (200 kph), jumpers drop about 764 feet (233 m). In just five seconds, they fall a distance that is greater than the distance from the top of the Washington Monument to the bottom.

House on the Rock Carousel

The world's largest carousel is in Spring Green, Wisconsin. The ride is 80 feet (24 m) across and is so big that it holds 269 carousel animals. One catch: People are not allowed to ride them! They can only watch this amazing ride spin around and around.

Rue Le Dodge

Rue Le Dodge is the world's largest bumper car ride. It is located at Six Flags Great America in Gurnee, Illinois. The floor has a total of 6,455 square feet (599.7 square meters). That's bigger than a basketball court!

Prater Tower

The highest swing in the world is the Prater Tower in Vienna, Austria. Riders swing 385 feet (117 m) above the ground. That's higher than the top of the tallest tree in the world—a 379-foot (116-m) redwood growing near San Francisco, California.

GLOSSARY

amusement parks (uh-MYOOZ-muhnt PARKS) places where people go on rides and play games

attractions (uh-TRAK-shuhnz) things that draw people's interest

bungee jump (BUHN-jee JUHMP) an activity in which a person jumps from a height while being attached to an elastic cord

capsules (KAP-suhlz) the parts of some amusement park rides where people sit or stand

chute (SHOOT) a steep slide

drop ride (DROP RIDE) an amusement park ride in which passengers are dropped quickly from the top of a tall tower

electromagnet (i-*lek*-troh-MAG-nit) a temporary magnet formed when electricity flows through a wire that has been wrapped around a piece of iron

geysers (GYE-zurz) holes in the ground through which hot water and steam shoot up in bursts

gondola (GON-duh-luh) the part of some amusement park rides that transports passengers into the air

hovers (HUHV-urz) stays in one place in the air

lagoon (luh-GOON) a small body of water that is partly or completely separated from a larger body of water by a small piece of land

model (MOD-uhl) a copy of something

pace (PAYSS) the speed at which something moves

plunges (PLUHN-jiz) falls steeply or sharply

raft (RAFT) a rubber or wooden craft with a flat bottom that travels on water

rotation (roh-TAY-shuhn) one complete turn or spin

structure (STRUHK-chur) something that has been built, such as a house or bridge

INDEX

BIBLIOGRAPHY

O'Brien, Tim. *Ripley's Believe It or Not! Amusement Park Oddities & Trivia!* Orlando, FL: Ripley Entertainment (2007).

Samuelson, Dale, and Wendy Yegoiants. *The American Amusement Park.* St. Paul, MN: MBI (2001).

Trabucco, Pete. *America's Top Roller Coasters & Amusement Parks.* Mustang, OK: Tate (2009).

READ MORE

Goldish, Meish. *Heart-Stopping Roller Coasters (World's Biggest).* New York: Bearport (2010).

Lepora, Nathan. *Marvelous Machinery: Rides at Work.* New York: Gareth Stevens (2008).

Mitchell, Susan K. *Amusement Park Rides.* New York: Gareth Stevens (2010).

Mitchell, Susan K. *The Biggest Thrill Rides.* New York: Gareth Stevens (2008).

LEARN MORE ONLINE

To learn more about amazing amusement park rides, visit
www.bearportpublishing.com/SoBigComparedtoWhat

ABOUT THE AUTHOR

Meish Goldish has written more than 200 books for children. He lives in Brooklyn, New York, near the amazing amusement park rides at Coney Island.